Ashley Escobar's *GLIB* is a brilliant debut, a tail-gating of versified New York forms for a joyride, knowing "death [will] come in cherry DumDum wrappers." Each dose props against the grips of being alive. Escobar's poems have "a carrier pigeon heart," a roving disposition, joys of early-life love, perpetual newness, "kisses in daytime television static," and memories where "we traded snowflake blisters." These poems are not blithe rumination, idle politic critique, nor tedious studies of cerebral inhabitance. Instead, they carry the breath that keeps one vital and moving, because with Ashley's poems "the world we write is the world we live in" and the effortless transience proves that details still light up the mind.

—Edmund Berrigan

Ashley Escobar's *GLIB* is a love letter to a pundit's bite — with a rapier-quick ear Escobar illuminates cultural artifacts like star systems on speed dial, "I'm a Post Beat It girl," implicating algorithms as post-party mantras with effortless ennui, "Is this Twee, is this avant-garde?" Every encounter is her muse, walking a lenticular language where motion is in the details, "where cold winter air is honest air." Escobar captures the bliss of a poet's burden with, "I don't know how I feel, about being everything," a Polaroid reckoning that refuses spectacle. *GLIB* is an effortlessly tender yet razor sharp debut, claiming, "aren't we the blueprint?"— indeed, our walk with hers, just started.

—Edwin Torres

Ashley Escobar's *GLIB* is "laboring under the misconception that everything is cringe." Yet, beneath the late-internet speak and absurdist imagery, a lovely sincerity emerges. This sparkling debut—which takes us from Brooklyn to California to Berlin—crackles with wit and realness, heartbreak and desire.

—Anna Dorn

Published by Changes
www.changes.press

Copyright © 2025 by Ashley Escobar
Foreword copyright © 2024 by Eileen Myles
All rights reserved

FIRST EDITION

Design by Studio Vance Wellenstein
Manufactured in the United States of America

Changes Paperback #006
ISBN: 979-8-9889042-8-1
Library of Congress Control Number: 2024937541

Ashley D. Escobar

GLIB

Foreword by Eileen Myles
A Changes Paperback

Glibbest of the GLIB

The main reason you're holding this book & I'm writing about it is that I couldn't stop reading. I had a pile of manuscripts around my knees (probably actually by my side or on the coffee table in front of me or on the floor but there's something more liquid about them being around my knees) and a bunch were good but the one called *GLIB* made me keep wondering what was next. But you know it wasn't actually even a thought. I just wanted to keep reading. I've read these poems fast and I've read them slow. It doesn't make any difference. They are very crowded poems, there's lots of stuff but I don't get full. It's like a forest in which one tree is painted and that's the end. I suspect I'll try to analyze why these are good, give a few examples and I'll just give up. Cause this work really is, and I'm grateful for that.

A one-page poem, a kind of wide one called "Premiere" nearly ends on this line: "Am I the Poetry Project of the film world." It's a thought. It's a funny thought. I don't even exactly know what it means and it doesn't matter. She might have said it to the person next to her in a screening. More likely she thought it. She could have written it in her notebook. That would make sense. Being the poet alone in room full of other kind of people watching a movie. But the final line is this—"that really was a quick Q&A." It's an aside. It's an about thing. It makes the room real by this relational line, again she didn't have to say it to anybody but it's an as if. But there's a gap between the two lines and that gap is poetry. You can't explain it at all but you know it in your gut. One line is a balloon full of air and one line is flat. And that transition gets you out of the poem and closes the experience. But in a really not trying hard way. It's just kind of hey. But you know what. That is the hardest thing in the world to do. And I still don't mean it's hard. It's just people don't do it perfect and she really does it a lot. There's something very unerring going on here. In all different ways. Why do I love "couch surfing / in my own apartment" so much. The poem kind of skedaddles, kind of wanders after that but towards the end (which is soon, same page) she goes "the suburbs are not / the end of all things // I am. That double slash doesn't really describe the loud amount of space between the two lines. The "I am" is almost floating on its own. But full of lonely power. What I can't convey here is the timing of the poem which is spatial and comic in a silent choked kind of way. I am worse than the suburbs it kind of says. But it doesn't say that at all. It just lets them hang out near to each other a bit.

I'll move on. I'm not sure I'm making my case. I actually know Ashley D. Escobar. And I knew her at the time I was judging. But I didn't know this was her. At all. It was the greatest joy to discover the "winner" was kind of a friend, a young acquaintance, a person I had sat across from the table from more than once. Maybe twice. So good news for everyone that you can be so close and yet so entirely far. I think I had read one poem of hers before. It was good.

"I do this, I do that. I steal saltine crackers." It's not necessarily one of her great lines but one I really like. One doesn't expect much from a send up of Frank O'Hara but Ashley has triumphed here by doing less. I personally love saltines but stealing them is not great. Or it is great. It just doesn't matter. It's a kind of slap. I think that's a part of what's going on. She makes these micro adjustments of order or kinds of discourse that end a chain of meaning so slightly. They provoke a mild what, it's like a bump, one of my favorite things in poetry. It's like the materiality of artifice that has to do with defining places as being here by the fact that so subtly you say they are no more.

Her poems are very thingy. That's what I meant by stuff. The world is constantly named. And framed. Also when I was saying that they don't make me full, I mean that even though there's streams and streams of references and details none really matter, the experience is how we glide through them swinging from vine to vine, that's why fast or slow it's exactly the same. You don't see more either way. It is the culture or cultures kinda. There's no inside, there's no outside. Here's this:

No actually this. The beginning of this poem is amazing. It's called "The Sprawl (Visited)"

> Every city in America
> looks the same. We are
> mountains hiding townies.

See, mountains and townies don't belong in the same poem, never mind the same line. It's impossible nature which is this poet. But here's where I was going.

> We don't

> know why we run away
> until that fragment
> of our lives is just
> an image of our

> white Crocs
> submerged in stormwater.

That's where the poem ends. And it's completely optical and completely emotional at once. Why are Crocs so silly. I might have them on my feet right now. I won't look down. But white ones are both fairytale and Katrina I think or the whole gigantic world of change. As we're pulling back further and further away.

"I remember I was seventeen for a year." We're in another poem now. I guess the joke is duration but it's also true. I wind up holding it her way which is Zen. I love that a poet who moves so much can almost anthemically proclaim

> I only
> know it
> in fragments

It's her movement that makes the fragments sing, her stillness that makes these lines … exist.

Altogether, she has to call it "glib" cause she couldn't call it wit, but it's absolutely that in a splattered age.

Sensibility, too.

— Eileen Myles

Post-Algonquin 1
Bob's Big Boy Parking Lot: 2:30 p.m. on Sunday 2
Adult Child at the MASS MoCA Kid Space 3
Nighttime at the Plastic Factory 5
Random Rules 7
Self-Portrait on Rue Bernard 8
I Dream in Bisquick 9
Cumbies Parking Lot Blues 12
Abortion Bitch 14
Having a Twisted Tea with You 15
On Penguins in Brooklyn 16
Mise En Scène 20
An Abode 22
The Sprawl (Visited) 23
Premiere 25
Vacation Noir 26
2/19 27
Joyride 29
April 31
Roey's 32
Potato of the Earth 33
July, in Past Tense 37

Poacher 45
Tivoli 47
Pleasant Street 49
Anyway 50
Beachcomber 51
On Sundays 53
I Dare You 55
Daddy 56
Wake Bake Get Laid 59
Love in the Afternoon 60
7/11 in Your Cat Eyes 61
Tripping Down the West Coast 62
Designated Passenger Princess 64
Morning Bath 65
New Heaven 67
Matt's New Notebook 69
Memory Babe 70
Night Hotel 71
Earthing 73
Toy Piano 74
Five Months on the Go 76
Acknowledgments 81

GLIB

I

Post-Algonquin
For Spiral

We are in the shop. The perfect functional beverage should have zero sugar or sugar alternatives. I am a sweetener stuck in perpetual genesis. I don't have ideas. I just have words. Cherry blossom La Croix tastes like a cherry cordial. Chocolates are for breakfast, but I don't eat breakfast out of contempt. Is noise dad rock? At least that's what Thurston asks me. I'd rather play guitar than write. I want to paint layers and layers of noise celestial sound. Whatever happened to Weldon Kees. I'm a Post Beat It girl. I drive Weldon's Plymouth Savoy into a lighthouse. I either create or curate chaos. I'm a speed walker fast talker soul stalker The "I"s I employ. The "I"s I destroy, dissect, control. I'm laboring under a misconception that everything is cringe. What isn't cringe. I'll speak in hieroglyphics. I'll be prolific after I get the decrepit cat to play piano. We are in the shop is our mantra. It's okay to be perfectly disgraceful. I'm perfect. Are you perfect. Walking in New York is like scrolling the internet. Woody's right about decay.

Bob's Big Boy Parking Lot: 2:30 p.m. on Sunday

Conversion, inversion, Christians & Luddites,
Devout, devotion, *Titanic Rising*, repeat,
Sacrilegious sugar, Smirnoff, mixed with Sprite,
Ashes to ashes, Highway 1 obsolete,
Devouring, devotion, Tinderless nights,
Tinder for fire, baby for hire, pulling teeth,
Drown in drought, Palm Springs, feeling tight,
Tighter wetsuit, coyote spotting, k-hole then k.
I face a billboard, waiting, have I seen the light?
To live and fry in LA, to live and die anyway,
Sisterhood of sister wives, sister tribes, hitchhike,
Pioneering for trust, silver screens, freshly fucked,
Dum Dum–stained lips, Donner Party gold strike,
Missing (Manson),
      back seat blowjob, Craigslist truck.

Adult Child at the MASS MoCA Kid Space

Spotted Mule.
Mad Dog Monkey.

Archival, revival.
As you arrive...

Have you ever catered
the last gathering

through a window?

      Do I walk?

Can I talk?

      Is that Kafka?

Or a large beaked moth?
Adult child, I—

My friend hears "the gays"
every time I say "the gaze."

I do more than eat hot chips and lie.
She doesn't know I want to kiss her.

She claims I'm afraid of butterflies.
I'm no good at counting.

I was underpaid at the curiosity shop,
Selling black diamonds to debutantes.

I haven't debuted to society.
I'm afraid the entrance will be premature.

I can't tell slopes from sides.
I skipped the math portion of the SAT.

Clean hands will damage the art.
I used to play four square in fourth grade

when I read *The Metamorphosis*
to seduce the school librarian.

She never thought I had brains.
I am a chalkboard. I am hazy.

Don't you hate when things are irregular?
I am unsure how a color band should behave.

I was put into therapy before I could tie my shoes.
Bunny ears sure beat the loopity loop.

Nighttime at the Plastic Factory

The Boys work in intervals - The Boys don't work - in plastic factories - hands slipping through automated machines - like my old friend - I could have sworn - their chapped lips touch - when I am not looking - and I always look - I have been looking for what feels like tomatoes - but only fifteen minutes have passed - since the last line of Focalin on his school-supplied desk - *White* by Bret Easton Ellis sitting next to strawberry Soylent - The Boys are skinny and mean - but we aren't opposites - we're twins on our way to temple on a nondescript Sunday - and the elder brother doesn't believe in God - he begins to question his existence - while we stampede the popcorn - littering the floor - it feels - packing peanuts - it feels - packing for college and knowing - this is it - it feels like intervals - we run out of tonic too early - we are clockwork - we are figures the other kids recognize - we don't sweep the popcorn dust - we kick someone else's white soccer ball to the other side of the hallway - everyone is fast asleep - and I wonder if it hurts when a jellyfish stings - if it hurts more because you know it's supposed to - The Boys say that jellyfish drift - that I'm a drifter - I've never been good at touching base - keeping my base safe - guarding it - that's the word I use when I run down the steps - my patent leather red heels - clacking against the wooden stairs - The Boys slide down the banisters - their navy Dickies covered in magnitudes of dust - Isaac offers me - a cigarette - but it's my twentieth - and I remind him I stopped smoking at seventeen - and he reminds me I am old enough to buy alcohol - that I am a spinster with graying hair in a Goodwill wedding dress - that I am - going to start smoking again - if I don't sleep with my professor - because old women don't say fuck - they say sleep - copulate - fornicate - gestate - but only until a certain age - they sew children's quilts out of teddy bear fabric - on a rocking chair - overlooking the Subway down the street - and a Dollar General - The Boys want to go - but it's closed on Sundays - and it's also 3 am - which means it's time to fill the jam jars - divide another line - and stop Teddy from drinking - leftover Diet Coke - in a McDonald's - Styrofoam cup - on Isaac's sick roommate's desk - Isaac doesn't care about the contagious stream - jam jars are our highest affectation - we don't have jobs - we have no idea what we do all day - except we do - it's clockwork - it's pretty easy - to unpack - when you live in your professor's closet - I share it with his part-time son - I wish I was his son - I am his cat - I could exist on his navy blue woven rug - for the rest of my life - if I could - it reminds me of being lost at sea - his youngest son asks - if I've seen his boat - but I don't see any nearby water - how could you lose a ship - in a landlocked place - Isaac says he'll visit me in the closet - but he never does - he keeps saying he'll stop drunk driving - and I believe him - because something about an old woman - holds hope - Isaac is so goddamn young - I can't be young - because I don't raw dog the world - I wear glasses to see - I drift with conviction - I drift toward death - I drift toward some girl Diana's room - after another line of white powdery chalkboard eraser dust - to steal her car keys - The Boys don't have licenses - we've never needed to drive - we walk out the bathroom window - to the rooftop - because it's 4:44 - and we like to sit on the chimney cap - and make a collective wish - whenever I am asleep on the woven rug - I get rudely awakened by - the youngest son throwing pennies at me - I am in a fountain - and I am the centerpiece - the statue - the muse - Isaac says if I were the muse - he would have finished his next novel - but he hasn't written in five years - I wish words were more - plastic - Isaac says - I could mold the letters easier - I could cut lines - I wish I were more plastic - so I never had to decompose - so The Boys never had to let go - of their gaunt little faces - like mini Rimbauds - with better haircuts - I fluff Teddy's hair - like cotton candy sheep at a carnival - and he asks if he thinks Isaac is - winking - back at us - pointing at the supernova - at a dying star - its last words painted blue - like the water sailor wives watch - from the tops of their houses - during the whaling days - waves lapping against the Atlantic shore - clockwork - unlike the supernova - whose explosion is a jaunt trip - it won't be light out until 9 - it won't snow for another couple of weeks - Isaac rolls down the eaves of the roof - I reach out to grab him - all I grasp is - cold - winter air - an honest air

Random Rules

Our neighbor tore down identical houses.
I scrubbed the bottom of the pool

with gelatin and ginger ale.
I vomited up a prophecy

in a dive bar inhaling hot dogs.
I quit smoking for the 112th time and lost

my liquor license to the tambourine player
who found ambition in a tropical fish tank

I broke when I wasn't high.
I divorced myself

from 8-balls and biblical names.
I was told I was too young

by a man who wouldn't let me
see his eyes.

People have lives.
What can I do about it.

Self-Portrait on Rue Bernard

Sunday best - at the Dollarama - I trace my footsteps - based on - the feather boas I see - I started having - linear dreams - in Montréal - I only know - the word Québécois - from the person who punched me - on the shoulder - in the shared parking lot - of a Dollar Tree and the local cinema back - in Bennington, Vermont - I booked - a ticket - knowing my death - would come in cherry Dum Dum wrappers and high gas prices - I use an Ampelmann umbrella - to stay dry - it's borrowed - the faux brownstones watch my leather coat - and leather Docs - I enter the toy shop - in hopes of - relieving - anxiety - the man at the counter claims - he's all out of duckies - I want Luckies - but I lost - two cigarette packs in a month - so I quit - *Would you like a dolphin instead?* - a set of twins - cross the street in grey school uniforms - one is taller - than the other - one's socks - are shorter - I don't buy anything - but a mental breakdown on aisle two - in between - a finger puppet - and a pregnancy test - I watch the cars - in between the toy shop - and the Dollarama - they take - their time - I want a heavy bus - to hurry past

I Dream in Bisquick

Sometimes my life is just being mad

at someone's younger sister and that's about it.

The toddler doesn't have a younger sister.

The toddler stabbed the cat with lefty scissors.

The toddler is right-handed.

I jump in my sleep.

I dream of eating Bisquick at a catered wide-tie party.

I wore heart-shaped sandals to class, and I had to change.

Heart-shaped sandals clash with brown corduroys.

I am an amateur tennis player crossing into Canada.

Someone tells me I can't be precocious as an adult,

but my preferred method of exercise is jumping jacks.

                                              Can I feed the toddler Bisquick?

                                            Is he going through a fish stick phase?

I take the toddler to the squid and whale diorama.

I pass by Noah Baumbach's house.

I've never seen a sperm whale.

I wonder what whale milk tastes like.

The Bisquick at the party is mixed with water.

They didn't have milk.

I asked for oat milk.

I like the texture of lumps of pancake batter down my throat.

The toddler asks for waffles on the way to the museum.

I want to do cartwheels to Bowie's "Modern Love" for all

of Brooklyn to see in scrunched-up ladies' tennis socks.

The giant squid is prey to the sperm whale.

I am both predator and prey.

Sperm whales still bear scars.

Salinger touched teenage girls.

Can I feed the toddler Bisquick?

We microwave fish sticks when we return.

Sperm whales use suction instead of teeth.

More sucking, less teeth.

We vacuum the cat hair off the blue rug.

The toddler arranges my funeral.

The toddler asks to be the flower boy.

I insist on ceremony.

His dad complains he's broke.

I have a habit of never reading

The New York Times Book Review.

Maybe the mailbox is the only place for this letter to exist.

I leave the trash can on fire.

Cumbies Parking Lot Blues

I am alone and
nostalgia isn't
what it used to
be. I don't pine

over memories

like a child
lamenting
a lost stuffed
whale. I drink
and forget
like how I'll
drink and forget

the sockless
man's foot.
I don't see

the hand that opens
the unlocked door.
The hand that lifts
my white skirt.
The hand that turns
into a fist.

I don't feel
blue anymore.
I don't shout
or scream.

The loading truck
backs up anyway.

I always thought
a gas nozzle looked
like a gun.

Abortion Bitch

I'm building a city
on my iPhone. Will you
throw the soup on Warhol?
My hands are tied by Lolita
hair ribbons. I'm moving into
a library. I'll sleep underneath
the signed first edition of *The Catcher in the Rye*
and steal stale popcorn from the cinema
next door.
   is this avant–garde?

Is this REI?
No, this is not REI.
"Did you just say this is REI"
We are in the shop. Kånken
no longer serves teenage art hoes.
Is this Twee
   is this avant–garde?

Is this improvisation
Is this jazz
Is this a revelation?
Is this a moving part
Am I a moving part?
Are we moving parts
of a tandem bike rolling
into the Central Park pond.
Why did people stop
being so beautiful?
Quit using the word
cinematic to describe
life. The Greeks didn't
have moving images. They spun pots.
Am I a moving image? I am three
years younger than Dorothy Parker.

Having a Twisted Tea with You

is sweeter than free focalin a stranger gives me
partly because we walked ten blocks and four
flights with the twelve pack   we're touching
elbows on a velvet green couch while my
roommate's door stays half open

partly because you have pictures of your
room on your phone to show me
in my room loitering and I don't know
         what color your eyes are until you bite
my lip on my sailboat sheets   they're fucking
                                                        blue

partly because you take off the tomato slice in your burger
partly because you tell me you don't like the taste of beer
partly because you still live at home and your mom won't
let you have the same clothing rack as me because she wants
you to have a desk   but you're illiterate

On Penguins in Brooklyn

    the protagonist feels like she's never leaving,
    stuck on a moving walkway
            in the middle of cincinnati
    international airport in kentucky, headphones dangling,
         she listens to mitski
               sing about writing sad songs

    twenty is too young
         to be at an airport bar,
              does this count as being in kentucky?

    the protagonist keeps forgetting she moved to brooklyn,
    the protagonist forgot about the olive farmer from spain,

        his red
            curls like bedsprings
    on valentine's day, but

        she doesn't forget
            about you,
    she reads.
        she read some sally rooney book, the one
    where the protagonist meets that married couple at a
            poetry reading, she keeps

    looking for you at every poetry reading but you're
    busy drinking seven dollar blueberry matcha tea in that
    new café by your brooklyn brownstone, the café that
        used to be a yoga studio that
            used to be a lightbulb store

    where she helped you pick out a penguin-shaped night light
        for your son's nursery

        your gelatinous
                wife didn't like it

your gelatinous wife never liked
        her, there aren't any penguins in
                brooklyn, but there were penguins
at the 21c hotel at the writers' conference you took her to

where everyone spoke on posing and voice and sally
rooney, the cluster of neon green penguins still haunts
        her, there are no penguins in brooklyn

there are bridges, do you ever
        think of the brooklyn bridge?

how twenty dead bodies are perpetually suspended
        in its granite towers
                while she's turning twenty-one in august, or
        is it only the queensboro bridge

fitzgerald promised you as the city's
        first wild promise, promises of
fistfight and fire escape, of glossier
        lip balm and you know that I've

never liked sally rooney
        but I've never told anyone that, like
I've never told anyone that your son still carries his stuffed kangaroo
rooney when he's forced
                to visit you those two weekends a month

you don't think two weeks is very long,
        but I tell you
it only takes two weeks to die of dehydration as you
        sip your blueberry matcha latte, I drink my coffee black,
                it makes you insecure

I wish
        I didn't have to attend poetry readings with your other
gentrifying friends, they keep asking me if I've received the new
sally rooney proof, your friends all work at fsg, that place that wouldn't
      publish your third novel and you
            had to outsource it in a foreign country

    I like the idea
        that there are penguins in brooklyn,
            and that you still text me

where are you? when I'm snorting coke at a party
    with the jonathans,
        franzen or lethem, never sure which one is which,
except one is friends with your mortal enemy, archenemies

    to lovers is your least favorite trope, we're definitely

tropes
like every sally rooney couple,
    like every phoebe bridgers song

I met the olive farmer in bushwick,
    you thought everyone in bushwick was an olive farmer,
but they were beekeepers, you always went boating on the atlantic,
    I've never liked the atlantic, their crosswords

are never hard enough, my friends think you can't get hard,
    I think it's hard whenever it's winter and I haven't seen you
for two weeks, and you remind me
                  two weeks isn't
very long, and you actually
              liked the new sally rooney book

you think it's her best one yet, but I think it's missing the bronx zoo,
because while there aren't any penguins in brooklyn, there are
    penguins in new york,
           and sally rooney
will keep pretending she's a college student

                              because she's deeply
   unhappy,

         and I will still be in brooklyn.

I saw one on my windowsill in a silver stovepipe hat.

Mise En Scène

I am deadpan delivery to your front door.
We'll kick soccer balls against the house
and talk about God. I hate being a figment
of the internet. I stole all the pretzels from
the party mix but eat nothing but
a folded Bemelmans napkin and sensibility.

I am writing a mumblecore film and a giraffe
will play the lead. We shook hands and scrolled
past the food, then check Twitter for the daily news.
I misunderstood your gluten intolerance.
I dropped a selfie for the algorithm
between the protest info and mutual aid.
Is my Brandy Melville insured?

I met a girl from Indiana who walks but can't
divine any meaning. I wash my face in an
unguarded puddle. I'd drink shots for breakfast
but Whole Foods is more than eleven blocks
away. Outside the window I see my friends
sleeping across Europe. I fed you a match
but you wouldn't take it. Jazz is cheaper
than water these days. We listen to last year's

songs in today's clothes. The mason jar
exploded but you can't see the coffee stain.
Let's talk to seagulls and commit to the bit.
I do this, I do that, I steal saltine crackers

for lunch tomorrow. I'd document my milieu
but I don't want a digital cowboy bootprint.
Who cares about slashes when you've got commas.

I am running away on the night train to Hudson.

I see false cities in the mountaintops, flickering
for reason. I only brought an umbrella and it
brought despair. I got so good at hide and seek
but no one wants to play. The kid next to me hands
over an olive chocolate almond. It's sticky and wet.

It must be Easter.
I collect people.
Monologues are cringe.
My teeth shift at night.
I answered a civic prayer in my sleep.
I was groomed to be a rockstar

but I caught a dizzying disease and hitchhiked
cross-country against my friends' ill-advised wills.
I am fighting fascists from my platform bed.
Sometimes I need noise, although I get tired
of everyone's voices. I was asked if I had a crush
on a guy or was just a junkie. Neither!

I forgot Joan Vollmer died when William Burroughs shot her.
I thought he just shot her.

My life changed the day I learned Burroughs became a writer after killing her.

Then I became a writer and stopped thinking about guns.

No one wants to loiter with me. I'll befriend the "No Idling" sign.

I shouldn't have turned on the jazz record.

I screen my film next to the gummy sour frogs.

      My walking song came on while I was standing.

The cashier thinks my life was stolen
but it was only memory

      and a two-dollar bill.

An Abode

We are neither winners nor saints. A man without
a face spreads his arms like a dove inside an empty
taqueria. It's raining and NyQuil helps me remember
my dreams. I don't think the candle belongs on
the board game. It belongs on Lou Reed or perhaps
Andy Warhol. Spiral thinks he looks embalmed
hanging on the wall, and I hear pillars dampen
the smell of decomposition. I'm his soldier child
of ecstatic consciousness subdued joy. I'm no corndog.
Am I a liar if I enjoy lying? I'M ANDY WARHOL
AND I NEED A HOUSE. I found a house, but I can't reclaim
the past. The books smell like incense.

The Sprawl (Visited)

Every city in America
looks the same. We are
mountains hiding townies.

I'm not a townie.
My mountains are malls.

I'm hippie-dippie
uptown but upstate

I'm too formal even as I
ash lavender cigarettes
into a Venus ashtray.

I left my purple tie-dye
shirt in California.
Mountains sprawl

behind the strip mall
health food store.

I balance my chakras
with pomegranate
& lemongrass & retox

with an olive roll
from Bread Alone.
I'm alone

on the train back
to Penn Station.

I'm no Holden Caulfield.
I don't lose things.
I protested my life

watching arthouse films
from a deconstructed
twin bunk bed.

These days apathy
has no purpose.
It's misguiding me.

I can't bear knowing
I won't outgrow
my spine. We don't

know why we run away
until that fragment
of our lives is just
an image of our

white Crocs
submerged in stormwater.

Premiere

Last stop - Matt's apartment - two blocks away - from the Chelsea - I'm Emma Roberts in *Adult World* except - not as naive - I wait until the end - of every open mic instead of going home - I never get - the dollar slice - I throw myself - on the ground - wrestle any floorboard until I get a nosebleed - and pretend I'm asleep - as he faces the wall - I once had a food Twitter but all food feels bland when you're full - I want to nibble on green olives - cheese cubes - and cornichons - and stop being yelled at by adults - Matt yells at me over Sunday night Frank Sinatra - but won't pull my hair - He's not into *that* - I'm into the Bright Eyes song - and collective prayer - I'm capturing currency - through melted chocolate coins - not Instagram lives - What about Hockney's New York - There are no new waves - only ocean - so I push him into the pool - He posts the blurriness I tried to capture - but I know the algorithm - won't share it with - my followers - I manipulate toy trains - and derail the Christmas tree - At least I don't have to deal with the consequences - What should I give up - for Lent - Liking the Pixies doesn't make you quirky - nor does going to a liberal arts school - but there's an overlap - I'll trade books for bread and butter - pickles - Am I the Poetry Project of the film world - That really was a quick Q&A

Vacation Noir

I watch the seagulls
on my dress and the bike
laughing at me I spilled
my guts to everyone you
can read the bible but
you'll never win the war
I strum the same three chords
expecting a new hurricane
on valentine's day two plus
two doesn't equal pink
neither does wearing
sunglasses to the club

2/19

hop off the train to boog city run into rachel

in her brown cowboy boots

  wish I had worn mine but I don't feel

tractor enough eddie

jokes about thurston thinking his

  father was a cult leader he doesn't

stick

around to watch me nibble

    on chicken fingers nowhere

crisp enough I could use some fries

why would you want

  to be commercial

    my instagram

is private for a reason

I went to berlin twice in a week

  on avenue a took the u-bahn at

moma fell asleep and chipped my tooth

        at the library   jukebox played

               the modern lovers

                      ironically saying

I'm straight

              over another amaretto sour

matt will claim   he lost

     his scarf   I hung it

around my adolescent limbs

Joyride

didn't cry   at the post office

it's february 24th

            & it's happening

again

    I laughed

        too hard at *blue velvet*

    kgb didn't deserve

        my twiggy makeup

couchsurfing

      in my own apartment

never coming

back to shore   drinking my way

    down

      ludlow

not enough

    dream logic

      these days

        should I

            fuck

up this deli sandwich

glossier you sticks to all cardigans

                the suburbs are not

the end of all things

                I am

April

I was walking down 2nd ave when the intangible turned tangible I thought I saw Frank O'Hara's ghost so I looked up at the trees they were all wearing sunglasses and the spaces in between the branches were spectacles of their own right Aidan told me to say *hi* to Frank but I didn't know him or maybe I did except I've never liked coke very much I'd rather have a pepsi and disappear I found myself in a brownstone with a bullet hole and the chandelier still wore all of its little hats as we climbed the ladder to Chelsea but were a few decades late *we don't serve cocktails until 4 p.m.* the neon hotel sign was my anchor, but I'm not a boat all my friends were postcards I licked their stamps half-heartedly so they wouldn't send but sometimes they'd go through I didn't want my worlds to mingle I guess that's called the post office writing can be tying the longest bow without occasion I wore ribbons in my hair and used to walk through the desert to get to the movies now I fall asleep during *ghost world* we did ketamine at the library and pocketed matching copies of *modern love* our names formed a slant rhyme as we drifted down the Bowery Matt called me stuffed animal terrier with a blank gaze inside jokes are experimental stand-up which makes me an experimental comedian *what's the color of the day?* it was always green and the opposite of tickle was steak and everyone said I looked like I drink martinis when all I want is a ginger beer I told Anselm to surprise me as he left for the store I tried writing a short story it started: if I had a middle name, it would be Lacuna if I had a cat, I'd name him Dog we'd even set it to music instead I wrote this poem I was waiting until I was old enough to remember then I cried to play on the swings and all I could see from the sky were hands touching, floating, shaking, dreaming, interwoven with magnolias and Matt promised we'd get ice cream but he got twinkies and I am nothing but a continued present

Roey's

I dream of
Matt's cock
at restaurant no. 3
between bites of Riviera
salad and garlic knots.
We end on Perry Street
overcoming our
mental breakdown on
the balcony of Popeyes.
We've sailed
in poetry since Thursday.
He lost his rolling
papers in Tompkins.
I think the mouse wanted
a drag. I'm glad I speak
to real mice
and not toy mice.
I can't handle self-
infantilization. I can't
handle targeted ads
for phone dolls
and conflating myself
with kittens and fawns.
I can't handle the West
Village without acid
flashbacks. I'm a morning
and an evening person.
Afternoons eat me alive.
I pocket the olive
he spits into my palm.

Potato of the Earth

i.

surprise applause
from the back
of backyard heaven
watch me eat a cherry
on public access television
chemical-free lipstick smear
along with diet coke
thirst rotting enamel
starling arrangement
hunched over a stratocaster
midlife crisis guitar
it's a six-drink minimum
& I've lost my drink ticket
to a stuffed whale

ii.

the wall stares back at me
olive lies head plopped up
can't make out malkmus
over the ac trembling syrup
fourth of july indoors fridge
wine lost all the ice cubes
to the sink dinosaur kale
lodged between teeth
when is dinosaur dream
time I play tambourine
funky our names form
a slant rhyme our forms
form a bedroom where
an intersection waits outside

iii.

he's getting his sleepies in
by the lightning bugs
if I had a million dollars
I'd get him a lifetime
supply of confetti cookies
but he'd scarf them all
in one sitting a morbid
one-act play that starts
in columbus ohio & ends
in central park maybe he
shouldn't have chosen
vodka tonic over a lime rickey
should've listened to february
in july instead he hit a lick

iv.

clog gaze pedal sounds
make aidan cover his
ears fingers sticky from
nonalcoholic bitters why
don't you mingle gen z
exposure therapy inside
billy's record shop east
williamsburg should just
be called bushwick what
do I know I'm a toy giraffe
with a hiccupping habit hush
for the next band do you have
the time I have the time off
its glancing at me sideways

v.

filip leads us
to the snack shack
out of the brambles
into the half moon
cherry lobster twilight
picnic under lightning
bugs and fireflies personal
preference pizza with pickled
pomegranates and oysters post
met pre-hamlet please don't
choke on the pearls I'm looking
for a lime rickey in a swimming
pool through this distortion I only
find whirls of pale pink against lace

vi.

coming and going
dropping your joint
first into a trash can
then off my balcony
leftover power bowl for
breakfast you know
you're allowed to eat
in my bed and clap
backwards to the cats
on the street the poet
onstage and I simultaneously
thought of blackout curtains
I wish everything was sheer just
text me when you're ready

vii.

girl dinner beside a
school bus I'd like
my peas pretty please
apple pay batsheva sailor
dress my beatnik buddy
is named henri not pierre
he's freewheeling not third
wheeling I found my book
of songs over my shoulder
breeding love in a box of
leftovers is hard enough
I'm waiting for the lights
to turn off so I can come
unseen undone unchanged

July, in Past Tense

I caught every day

        separately

with a different butterfly net.

    I woke up to the trees

    trembling

    outside my window.

I listened to "Imprint" by Felt on repeat
staring at my ceiling

      in bed, the light movement reminded me
      of something angelic
      I had once seen on shrooms, sun rays like halos.

I picked up my phone for only an hour or two each day.

I floated to and from the market
to buy one thing at a time

    first cherries

then a pint of whatever
ice cream was on sale,
or Spanish olive oil, whatever caught my eye.

    I got jealous

      of people making memes

    about the open mic

when I was using my hands to write a book, a play, about it

a laborious process worth

so much more than a quick laugh.
I let it go

at least they shared their art on stage.

    I started writing

    a series of sonnets

    labeled "Potato of the Earth" because I misspoke.

Paris and I

      had grown estranged.

The clouds were as colossal as I liked them.

When gloom entered my poetry nook, it reminded me
of any apartment corner in San Francisco. I almost heard
the MUNI bus whirring up the hill

      or teenage skateboarders rolling by.

I missed the fog.

    I befriended sailors
    in Prospect Heights
    over piña coladas.

I listened to poetry
in courtyards, a flock of birds
always created a chorus.

I thought of my book as a setlist but wanted to improvise.

    I was running out

    of happy hours

    but I would rather stay inside.

I dreamt of pools
and only speaking
to someone on long train rides.

I was careful of who I shared my portable picnic with.

    I hit a lick sometimes.

        I was bad at the saw, but it takes getting used to. I was a dog walker, but I didn't have a leash. I took new trains and got off randomly when I needed to dérive. I made myself espresso in a little moka pot and variations on scrambled eggs. I was creating an orchestra every morning out of chives, green onions, and shredded cheese. I stored cereal for the less ambitious days or the days I needed more of a crunch.

I stopped wearing a heart on my cheek.

I only wore dresses
or long flowy skirts.

I was covered
in mosquito bites.

        I let the lightning bugs

                              go

and watched the cat
nap every afternoon.

        I intertwined my body

        with yours

        when we found a moment alone.

                This brick façade is our arcade.

Poacher

Only tomorrow and today is today--
I watched you cut your hair on the first of false spring.
Standing behind the sink, rusty scissors over a vigil of starfish and glass,
I asked for baby bangs. You thought Mother had fixed the rickety swing.
Bit into a blue marshmallow bunny. Easter as silent as your curls in the litter. Dusk
evinces our mistrust of being anything less

than second-rate scavengers, dreaming of a sunset hue, hopeless,
caught in morning dew. Doomed to making sacraments every day.
Roaches stuck in pink bathroom tiles, fully clothed men unappeased by dusk.
I tried on the tie father left behind. Sacrificial honeymoon from my bedspring.
How serious can anyone be. I caught a glimpse of you on the porch swing,
kicking the tragedy, you looked like an opening by Philip Glass.

My sunflowers died first. Our cat allergic to your lilies, I traded the glass
for something warmer than your insides. Warmer than a rifle. Mindless
I pulsate in an air-conditioned room. Weightless. My mood swings
trade places with motherly instincts and sheer teddies until doomsday.
I remember brother, when your hair was long, when we played outside. Spring
came later than usual, braids to touch at dusk

when owls eradicated any sense of luck. Not that dusk,
the one before. Donny was quiet, he showed us sea glass
his mother had saved when she was a girl in a white dress in spring
and the only hints of snow were frosted animal crackers. Loveless,
Donny told us he could hear waves overcome him. Donny was on holiday
when he pulled up my white dress. He must have confused our swing

with those you find in b&bs. When I think of Florida, I don't think of our swing.
I think of palm trees and supermarkets, of wet sand, pink air at dusk--
Donny must have learned from you, to come inside, like you came yesterday
and Mother couldn't hear you over the sound of a smashing wine glass.
I tugged your hair but didn't tell you to stop, your crushing weight left me gutless.
Donny did not moan like you, his was softer than flowers thawing in spring.

I did not want change, for winter thoughts to melt into cruel springs.
Donny moving to Florida to capture those greens and blues. Us on the swing
under evening hues. I'm scared for you to learn to drive, to be hapless,
sucking as you steered. I let you, didn't I. Would you drive at dusk?
I have a carrier pigeon heart. Not yours, or Donny's. It belongs to windows and glass,
shadows behind my bed frame. I don't want to hear the word eggs today.

You cut your hair on my thirteenth birthday--
Donny used to call us twins, before he lost his sea glass.
When I thought I was a prophet of lost faith, every dusk.

Tivoli

Tulips waiting
to bloom
in schoolyards.

Children
in wellies

stomp

the alphabet
into the street.

Streetlamps
          bend over, I
am not yet a trampoline.

I'm pining
for a soon-to-be
stepmother of three.

Her
reflection meets mine

in a stale
puddle of milk.

All the town's
clocks died.

I missed
every train;

trains shouldn't
arrive
on the same track.

I'll eat
away her guilt.

I fought
in a war

I let her win.

Pleasant Street

We ate dinner at five pm

        and traded snowflake blisters.

Mine looked like a triceratops.

Threw nickels

        by the limestone quarry

                at Budweisers on the rails.

Talked about old dogs

        and the way they bite

                slowly hesitant then all blood lost remorse

I crushed Luckies on wailing grass

        licked the ice

(tasted chlorinated)   saw a lion on the face of a trashcan

                      and a baby on a pinwheel.

Looked for a job at the bowling alley.

                Found a flood at the bottom of a single saddle shoe

Anyway

today   & tomorrow's bliss
loneliness is watching trees

our time—a window, looking
out onto an   empty street

winter stretched its arms   open
we hid until the   blueness

caught us,   gravitate toward
distance   (silence)   sit & stare

february   nearly killed
you, dawn is no longer mine

our repentance holds what we
keep unsaid   our dreams stay pure

owls are no longer strangers
night fall   reflects in your eyes

everything here is slowly
turning   (patient in the rain)

and the   trees stand like people
and the people will stand like   trees

Beachcomber

If nihilism is your punishment then
Sisyphus would be envious

of your ravenous behavior,
sluiced in a milky white texture
        after dark. My deliquescent heart is
asphodel. The tenacious sunset bears witness
to our leisure. Maudlin and silent,
a helpless lark summons me to stay.

Debauchery is purely
        episodic. Interconnected vignettes of a past life
taunting your slumber. Momentary saturnine bliss to
feed the skinny city foxes. Berlin has left me naked on a
train station platform. I dropped my sundae because I was high

I hunt a deer in my sleep, she is a quiet
clever thing. A week without sowing, a week
        without dreams. I cook tomorrow's stew in your mother's
enamel pot—venison braised in an acerbic melting pool of
cream. I hover over her, an apparition, it makes me feel small
like a bank of swans from a tall bridge. A currency lost in translation

Our parapet holds centuries of mystery, I hold
onto the daisies left by my bedside.
        The houses by the sea stay the same muted colors,
robin egg blue and pale olive green. A lethargic silence drools over
us. One that only arrives past midnight when cars sound like tidal
waves and waves feel like static. It's a maggot-filled holiday

It is bee sting cake on a bittersweet Sunday, clover
fields emptied for cows to graze. Purity is reserved
      for strangers. I was never tall enough to meet
your gaze. Beckoning overseas with a cigarette between
each knee. It is time to wake up, to get going, but you
are paler than heaven. This is becoming, not being

A sinuous evening, I cradle my fishnets behind the
front door. Somnambulism takes you over
      by day. I find a broken seashell in my comb. Our eyes
adjust to the light, concrete never felt so good. Every
era, saccharine and stale. I run past my own
                                       fingertips

On Sundays

The past slithers to me

        from a corner booth.

My milkshake melted before

        the pink could reach my lips.

My past lost hours of sleep

        like the fork I left on a red picnic table upstate.

All I had was a white convertible to chew corn nuts

        and smoke chamomile joints in, driving

drunk was your specialty along with kissing

        foghorns in the dark. I was a sailor

valentine one week too soon. I heard it rained

        artificial tears in California.

You complained you couldn't read

        your hands too dry for comprehension

but I read the diary you left

        against the moldy clementines

dated back to butterfly clips and my runny nose.

       I was a translation of a dream

Long summer feelings

       dissipate eventually.

(You let all the peonies die on the windowsill)

       A message underneath the split pea soup reads:

(WEDNESDAY ONLY)

I Dare You
after Tilly Losch

I pilfered

        a life without

                strings

deceived by

        lacewings,

                how delicate

how serene.

        I borrowed a puppet

master to teach me

        how to fly.

I floated like a

        circus tent

over sand dunes,

        under crescent moons.

Strike me!

        I refuse spectacle,

                yet through flames—

I become someone else's sun.

Daddy

I made
a diorama

with your
name on it

The subtle
violence

of a
knife

left alone
on an orange

next
to an aging goose

A loose thread
falls off

my ribbon

onto your
homemade hair

I am
a streetwalker

except
for when
you come

on my face

I call this
a mumblecore film

trapped

between

sailboat sheets
and a stuffed beagle

We tilt
our heads

in the same direction
on Photo Booth

pink heart
halos follow

our every move

Why don't
you stop

going to sleep
at 4 a.m. and stop
waking up at 4 p.m.

to smoke weed

Let me staple
your zines

and dictate
your emails

I am your
secretary

I am on
my best behavior

I have been many
places but my legs

don't tire

around
your waist

You call me
a toddler

yet grab my ass
in the kitchen

Your dick
is my favorite toy

and I hate sharing

Let's buy
another eighth.

Wake Bake Get Laid

Everything - is orange - I am your unresolved - sonnet - Let's get a shot - of my existential ennui - on the second floor - of Duane Reade - These are the end times - East Coast wildfire - season to follow - train derailment - The stores have run out - of mini - composition notebooks - but I am an ongoing diary of a teenage girl - I am from San Francisco - but not the sixties - I grew up on Pizza Hut - and Juuls - I was forced into Discord - and discourse - This is the summer - of cold brew - rolling joints - and ignoring - calls from Artnet - because you're too busy - binging Woody Allen - and fucking - a twenty-two-year-old - We are wild at heart - I simultaneously - wear bell-bottom jeans - and an American Apparel tennis skirt - It depends on how you turn - the kaleidoscope - We interloped - at the right time - I play tambourine in our imaginary band - and record your stand-up routines - There has to be a future - Your bite mark - hasn't left my right arm - I forgive you - for not eating - your half - of the shroom - Just leave a spot - for me - in your diary

Love in the Afternoon

My negligee struggles to stay on.
You let it fall along with the paper elephants
on my wall. It's our Éric Rohmer summer.
Summer without a pool, but let's change that.
The shadows embrace our ennui, and I
embrace your tenderness. I was imprisoned
by thought until we met the city in the rain.
I love being alive with you.

7/11 in Your Cat Eyes

I threaten to drive
everyone under the geyser
at Echo Park in a white swan
        think we'll drown,
sleep on the hazelnut floor
next door to Hockney's pool
overshadowed by poplar trees.
We are a school of fish.
Fish in an Eileen Myles way
Impish. Waifish. Superficial
You drive me to get vegan
frozen yogurt despite eating steak tartare.
        I want a Slurpee and a cigarette.
No more lunchtime Luckies
You don't even smoke.
        Summer tackles us
onto the curb in our tennis skirts.
Someone calls us groupies
        Aren't we the opening act?
I know my mom hates LA but I wish
she was here to drive through Big Sur.
        I think I know exactly
what'll happen to us in five years
but I probably don't

Tripping Down the West Coast

I met a guy		who lived in Mexico City.		Said it had more

		comings and goings	than New York.		I believed

him because he was the kind			of stranger I ran into

every now and then		without		any contact otherwise.

I was searching for flames			in a paper dollhouse. We only

congregate outside bars		over cigarettes or someone's leftover

joint		until nine months pass		by and we recognize each

other's reflection		under a dim	streetlamp after hours.		I was

hoping		he'd help me find a match		but he drifted around the corner

before I could ask.		I kept picturing		how my window must look

when evening comes		unannounced.		Your silhouette

crouched behind a sheer curtain		in a now empty room.		Summer

used to feel like an eternity.			Another kid came into view.

		I know him!

He's in a band		called Now and lives in a world

where it is always burning noon.

	It all boils down to *The Abortion*

                    by Richard Brautigan except

         you work at a cabaret instead   of a library.

This is our historical   romance circa 2023.   If you were

         here, you'd be a hero in Berkeley.   He asked me how community

college was in paradise.   I told him   I memorized this city

         block as a child

                  but we've since grown

estranged.   His lighter

         gave out.   I got up and walked

                                                   somewhere closed.

Designated Passenger Princess

I have a tepid affair with
California. Everything sounds
cooler taken out of context.
The progress of love
does not feel triumphant. I left
my heart alongside the devil
and Daniel Johnston driving
to an anagram for nowhere
to buy a strawberry smoothie
named after a celebrity.
I used to have an elephant too.
I skipped my dad's remarriage
to watch Godard's *Contempt*
and sneak into a Weezer show.
Is Weezer avant-garde?
I pull the glass to release
the imaginary fish. I was born
again on the party bus
to Chuck E. Cheese in a bright
pink wig when all I had
were quarters for the jukebox
and an intuition that you were
me. We're back for season two
but my carrier pigeon is in Rome.

Morning Bath

Sometimes
I remove

my glasses
so I can't see

farther
than your face

I grasp at my neck
as a reflex

but the long
lock

of your
hair hasn't

made its way
here yet.

Reading Ashbery
out loud

in the lobby of the Met
I feel like a kid again.

Pulling weeds
without consequence

I litter them all over
your striped shirt.

Sometimes I fear
you'll leave

while I'm in the shower

but you're still
rolling another joint.

I want to travel
in the back pocket

of your blue jeans
until childhood

finds a new name.

There are no new
tears, only me

and an extended-release
lavender bath bomb.

I'll cry until
all the water

drifts down the drain.

New Heaven

October jangles

                into my ear   in the parking lot

of Brick Oven Pizza.   Three girls sit on

      someone else's convertible

                singing along to Kiss.

We're not going

              on a joyride.

We have nowhere to be.   Standing

      on chopped-down trees

              in the soft glow

of angel numbers

           I feel dizzy and illogical

I wouldn't mind   walking straight into

      the ocean.

                To fall

      ill in your arms.

My nose

        is already colder than yours.

I keep trying   to capture

        the prayer

but it's already   been caught.

        No one knows

        I'm still here.   I was made

        for being your fawn.

I used to write   short stories when I used

        to think   when I used to have

people

        to think with   remember

the diner   won't remain

        closed forever.   I don't

want to know

        if he takes

        the drunk girls home.

I'm the one with the bite marks.

Matt's New Notebook

I point at the floating dinosaur on Matt's new
notebook where we will write our hit play.
I am disillusioned by my shadow.
If I follow a glib statement with another
glib statement will it begin to make sense?
I remember I was seventeen for a year.
I shivered and it felt like high school.
I used a phonebook as a stepladder. Back
then, I feared ladders and walking under them.
I huddled under my covers listening
to Lou Reed. I wore the right day of
the week. I walked my cat named dog.
I wove museums out of fog.
I hadn't begun to dream in Polaroid
yet. Matt took back my birthday
present. I thought there were no
takebacks. Only callbacks.
For Lent, I'm giving up reading. I'd still
like to improvise, but I can't reach
my viola. I'm busy sobering my body
in the cold next to his. We're softies.
Everything in New York is flat except
for this hill I am on and the hill is
my house. Strangers would come
in and out of my room. Told me I should
keep the music on. So I did.

Memory Babe

losing it

laughing

        everywhere

and anywhere is prohibited.

semblance
of style and I

larping the art

        school kids

we were a mere two years ago.

dachshund of my youth

museum glass
at my feet

I am every
matinee   of your heart.

reading slow

as a form of   elongation.

I don't want
a lot
        just forever

Night Hotel

Can you livestream
in the night hotel?

I'm waiting   for you in pigtails
and a tennis skirt. I'm at the foot
of everyone's midlife crisis.

We're in a post–Bret Easton Ellis world
          the world we write is the world we live in
wasn't that the New York School?

I'd have a Coke with you
but your teeth would rot.   Your teeth
are most precious   a neighborhood of
pre-gentrification dive bars to smoke inside.

People are afraid
to merge but this isn't a freeway.
There are no signs
          of life besides the bellhop.
We don't have bags, only desires.

Drive us into the Hudson
in a rented Jaguar as I give you head.
          My teeth stay hidden.
Followers will theorize
our disappearance. Found footage conspiracy

Norman Fucking Rockwell
was born
      a few blocks away. You're buying an eighth
for fifteen. I'm drifting toward room service.
I would go out tonight, but my phone
isn't charged.
      I would go out tonight, but when
you return, we'll just fall asleep.

Earthing

The first thing I feel
when I wake up is your hand
over my face. We love
long films and poems but the search
is more entertaining. Yes, the express
jump from 72nd to 42nd
is the hardest part of leaving.

Someone tells me that my breast
is out for all of Bleecker Street
to witness. Where's Matt
to put it back for me. I want to nap
on the highest branch. I worry
that the black coat in the courtyard
is yours but you left it at home. I'll never
let them turn the whole city into Murray Hill.

Apparently I still cross the road
like I don't know where I am.

I am kissing you in a landscape
and everyone has accidental
flowers in their hair. We earth
next to the azaleas as April gives us
her final showers. You understand
that I am the poem and the one writing it.

I, steadfast,
a statue amongst dreams

Toy Piano

I won't be ready

      when you come around.

I can't stop   listening to shoegaze or wearing Mary Janes in the rain.

My socks are pastel pink

      with tiny cherries. I'm cherry-flavored

                                everything.

I'm culturally significant.   I threw up

                    on the KGB stairs and performed after.

Drop kick

      my life. Pretend I don't have scurvy.

I knew a kid who believed

      he had it. Blamed me for not

            saving him from the cliff.

I was a coyote

      eating blackberries.   Talking feels like clawing

through the brambles.   I hung   dried flowers on the wall

      ate all the loose petals now   I eat walls.

I am both sign

       and the signified   We went on a road trip

but neither of us knew how to drive   past

       sprawling lawns of highlighter-yellow toys

and frisbees   It's August

              in this dream   and the next

Five Months on the Go

I find new songs from old ones "five months on the go"

by Dear Nora came on once "To Fall Is Not to Fail" ended

then followed me on the train as pale pink clouded the sky

the houses along the Hudson remind me of Half Moon Bay

I want to read the boat names but they're still covered for winter

Only trees reveal themselves

We finished *Palo Alto* at 4 am because of daylight savings I was asleep

for most of it I had too much pride to admit I was high so I stared at a blank page

five months on the go and I don't know where I am right now

I was on this 5:14 train in October I had just met a poet who never replied

to the playlist I made him I didn't know Bernadette Mayer back then

couldn't find *Grapefruit* so I settled for *Acorn* did sky piece from the ground

whispered my name to a pebble Penelope still has it I told the poet I want to

intertwine music

with the intimate

Our soundtrack's coming from my Marshall speaker an underground

bunker in Williamsburg El Quijote's overhead sound system the poet's PA

KGB Red Room, Penelope's car, her Alexa, Lenny Kaye at The Algonquin

my world is turned upside down

Last time, we went to Bread Alone I didn't know who I should be

for Halloween the poet declined Bella Ciao and played the SNL closing song

I went home as Annie Hall and closed my eyes to wake up for school every adult

sounded like one on *Charlie Brown* I threw muffins at the wrong people

November led to sharing the poet's futon I did everything *for the bit*

waited for the year to pass I saw the poet's noise show but

that was sincere I was the only one who danced

in San Francisco I retraced the steps that I took when I was younger

up Noriega and Haight on the bus then I stepped out into the fog

I got a pin that reads: Outpatient at the Teenage Art Ward

back home in the fog

I only

know it

in fragments

strawberry lemonade ketchup stains bonfire minus the fire waiting

fifty-five degrees may as well be spring skin contact is what they call

orange wine but we go for the white I found a use for color I haven't

written anything honest in five months with NyQuil-stained lips I finally

doubled the children's dose I keep a gold star around my neck

it's my only consistent trait I spent hours in coffee shops pretending

to work now all those coffee shops are closed I can't climb the tidal

waves at the park anymore I annoy my friends at Amoeba why

didn't I bring my fish pants?

I forgot that I can

tickle someone

I woke up to the poet on my twin bed with my heart transferred

onto his temple he called my music twee I whistled in the same color

as New Year's Day overlooking a waterfall I'd like another tuna sandwich

my world is turned upside down

I reassembled my childhood with Eddie at 12th Street

Ale House we laid out the ocean with our hands

I like the long beep when my dryer ends

Beeeeeeeeeeeeeeep

Acknowledgments

Thank you,

Hobart, *The Drift*, *The Brooklyn Rail*, *A Gathering of the Tribes*, *TRANSOM*, *berlin lit*, *ExPat Press*, *Easy Paradise*, *Ethel zine*, *Lonesome*, *Unresolved zine*, and Invisible Hand Press for publishing some of these poems.

Mom, for everything, especially all the trips to the library.

Cuthwulf Eileen Myles, for getting it.

Easy Paradise and the Poetry Project at St. Mark's Church for making New York City my home.

My teachers, close readers, and friends: Edwin Torres, Filip Marinovich, Michael Dumanis, Anselm Berrigan, Julien Poirier, Jeffrey Joe Nelson, Noah Jacobs, Kaya Lau, McCaela Prentice, and Lauren Caldwell.

Everyone at Changes, especially Bennet Bergman.

Kyle Dacuyan for your patience and kindness; you were a dream editor.

Eddie Berrigan, for feeling tractor.

Kendall Peterson, for writing a poem every day for a month with me in the haziness of October 2020.

Lulu Bernal for being outside my Berlin apartment.

Matt Proctor for coming up to me in my pink wig. I love being alive with you. Let forever stay belated.